The Let's Talk Library™

Let's Talk About
When a Parent Dies

Elizabeth Weitzman

The Rosen Publishing Group's

PowerKids Press

New York

Published in 1996 by The Rosen Publishing Group, Inc.
29 East 21st Street, New York, NY 10010

First Edition

Photo credits: Cover photo by Guillermina DeFerrari; p. 20 © Earl Kogler/International Stock; all other photos by Guillermina DeFerrari.

Weitzman, Elizabeth.
    Let's talk about when a parent dies / Elizabeth Weitzman. — 1st ed.
         p.   cm. — (The let's talk library)
    Includes index.
    Summary: Provides advice on surviving the death of a parent and suggests what feelings and behavior to expect from others.
    ISBN 0-8239-2309-6
    1. Children and death—Juvenile literature. 2. Parents—Death—Juvenile literature. 3. Bereavement in children—Juvenile literature. 4. Grief in children—Juvenile literature. [1. Death. 2. Grief. 3. Parent and child.] I. Title. II. Series.
    BF723.D3W44 1996
    155.9'37—dc20   96-3335
                                                                              CIP
                                                                              AC

Manufactured in the United States of America

Table of Contents

Marisa

When Marisa was eight, the worst thing she could ever imagine happened: Her father died. At first, she didn't believe it. "No!" she yelled, pushing her mother away and running up to her room. She knew it was a lie. Her father would never leave her. He loved her too much.

Marisa's father did love her with all his heart. But no one can **control** (kon-TROLL) death— or the feelings that it causes.

◀ You can't control how you feel when your parent dies.

Grief

You will experience many confusing feelings after your parent dies. You may even wonder if something is wrong with you. But these feelings are normal. Most people who lose someone they love feel a sadness so strong it has its own name: **grief** (GREEF). Grief is a very strong emotion. Feeling grief is called **mourning** (MOR-ning). It may be hard for you to believe things will ever get better. They will. But it may take a long time.

It may be hard to believe now, but your feelings of sadness will start to go away one day. ▶

It's Not Your Fault

Like other kids, you may blame yourself for your mother's death. You may wonder why you didn't clean your room as she asked, or why you fought with her that last time. And you may not remember when you last told her that you loved her.

But nothing could ever make a mother forget that her kids love her. A parent's death is never a punishment. You are *not* to blame.

◀ *Nothing* that you did or didn't do caused your mom to die.

You Can Never Love Too Much

Now that your father is gone, you may think things would be easier if you hadn't loved him so much. You may decide to stop loving everyone so it won't hurt as much if someone else dies. But this will just make everyone—especially you—feel much worse. Right now you need to give and get as much love as you can.

You may not know it, but you need love now more than ever before. ▶

A Common Fear

You may be afraid that your other parent will die too. But it's very rare for children to lose both parents. In fact, it's so unusual that you should try not to worry about it.

But remember that no matter what, there will always be other family members and friends who will make sure that you and your sisters and brothers are loved and taken care of.

◀ You will always have friends and relatives who love you and will take care of you.

13

Changes

There may be many changes in your life after your father dies. You may not get new toys or an allowance for a while, because your family needs to save money. Your mother may have to work harder and get home later.

Try to help out around the house. If you do a few extra chores, it will make things easier for your family. It may even help keep your mind off your sadness for a little while.

There are lots of things you can do to help, such as folding your clothes. ▶

Share Your Feelings

You've never felt this way before. You may think that nobody else has either. You probably feel very alone. But many people have felt grief over the death of someone they love.

Talk to a family member or friend about how you feel. A teacher, a minister, or a rabbi will listen and understand too. Because one good way to feel better—and less alone—is to share your feelings.

◀ Sharing your feelings with someone may help you feel better.

Acceptance

After your mom dies, it may seem as if she's still there with you. You can still smell her perfume. And every time the door opens, you may think it's her, walking in as if nothing's happened. But then you remember that she is not coming back.

These feelings can be very painful, but they are normal. After a while they will start to fade. You will begin to accept that your mom is really gone, and then things will get easier.

You will never forget your mom, but the pain of missing her will start to go away. ▶

The Next Step

Many months—maybe even a year—after your father dies, your grief will start to fade. When this happens, you'll be able to think of him and smile. It's hard to imagine now, but you will want to have fun again.

Your father would want you to be happy. So when you're ready to join your friends on the playground or at the beach, remember: Your dad would be happy to see you laughing again.

◀ One day you'll be ready to smile and laugh again.

Memories Last Forever

What happens after someone dies is a **mystery** (MIST-er-ee). However, there is one thing you can be sure of: Your parent will never completely leave you. As long as you have **memories** (MEM-or-reez) your mother or father will stay in your heart for the rest of your life.

Glossary

control (kon-TROLL) Have power over something.

grief (GREEF) The feeling of anger and sadness after someone has died.

memories (MEM-or-reez) Things you remember about someone.

mourning (MOR-ning) Feeling grief over someone's death.

mystery (MIST-er-ee) Something that can't be explained.

Index

A
acceptance, 18

B
blame, 9

C
changes, 14

D
death, 5, 6, 9,10, 13, 17, 22

F
fear, 13
feelings, 5, 6, 17, 18

G
grief, 6, 17, 21

H
helping, 14

L
loneliness, 17
love, 5, 6, 9, 10, 13, 17

M
memories, 22
money, saving, 14
mourning, 6

P
parent, death of, 5, 6, 9, 10, 13,14, 18, 21, 22

S
sadness, 6, 14

24